A CARIBBEAN COUNTING BOOK

ONE WHITE SAIL

Words by S.T. Garne
Pictures by Lisa Etre

HARCOURT BRACE & COMPANY
Orlando Atlanta Austin Boston San Francisco Chicago Dallas New York
Toronto London

This edition is published by special arrangement with Green Tiger Press, an imprint of Simon & Schuster Inc.

Grateful acknowledgment is made to Green Tiger Press, an imprint of Simon & Schuster Inc. for permission to reprint *One White Sail* by S.T. Garne, illustrated by Lisa Etre. Text copyright © 1992 by Simon & Schuster; illustrations copyright © 1992 by Lisa Etre.

Printed in the United States of America

ISBN 0-15-302106-3

3 4 5 6 7 8 9 10   035   97 96 95 94

One white sail
on a clear blue sea,

Two orange houses
and a slender palm tree,

Three girls walking
with baskets of bread,

Four boys skipping
on the trail to Ram's Head,

Five blue doors
in the baking hot sun,

Six wooden windows
let the cool wind run,

Seven old men
on a sparkling white beach,

Eight pink clouds
dancing just out of reach,

Nine steel drums
sing a soft sweet tune,

While ten boats sleep
'neath a pale island moon.

The illustrations for
ONE WHITE SAIL are
rendered in watercolor.
The text is set in
Avant Garde Extra Light.